David and Goliath

By Christin Ditchfield
Illustrated by Jerry Smath

A GOLDEN BOOK • NEW YORK

Text copyright © 2019 by Penguin Random House LLC.
Cover art and interior illustrations copyright © 2019 by Jerry Smath.
All rights reserved. Published in the United States by Golden Books, an imprint of Random House Children's Books, a division of Penguin Random House LLC, 1745 Broadway, New York, NY 10019. Golden Books, A Golden Book, A Little Golden Book, the G colophon, and the distinctive gold spine are registered trademarks of Penguin Random House LLC. rhcbooks.com
Educators and librarians, for a variety of teaching tools, visit us at RHTeachersLibrarians.com
Library of Congress Control Number: 2017946463
ISBN 978-1-5247-7109-6 (trade) — ISBN 978-1-5247-7110-2 (ebook)
Printed in the United States of America
10 9 8 7 6 5 4

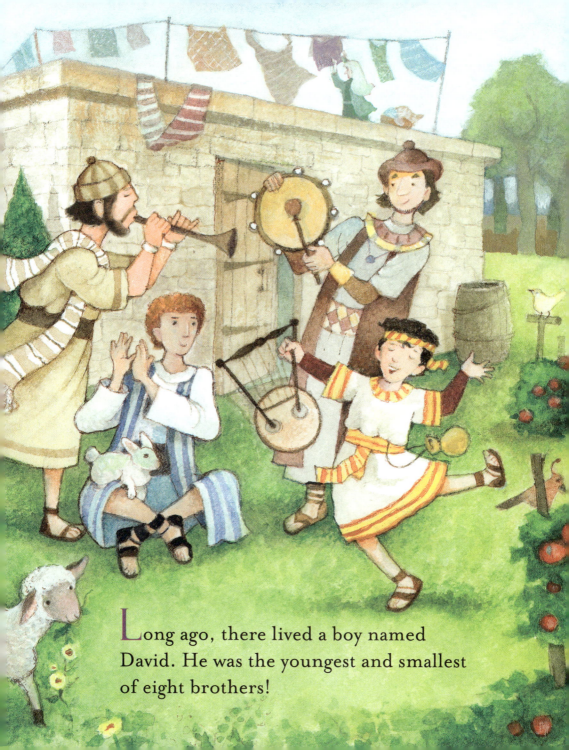

Long ago, there lived a boy named David. He was the youngest and smallest of eight brothers!

David's father put him in charge of watching over the family's sheep. Most of the time, things were quiet in the pasture. While the sheep were grazing, David often practiced hitting targets with his slingshot.

He also talked to God about his thoughts and feelings—anything and everything in his heart. And he made up songs thanking God for His beautiful world.

One day, David's father gave him an important job to do. He wanted him to take food and supplies to his older brothers, who were soldiers in King Saul's army. They were camping on a battlefield nearby.

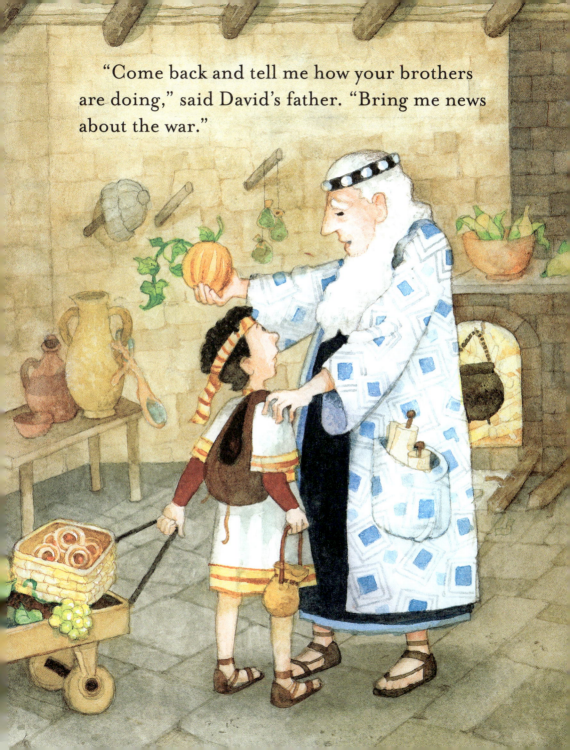

When David found his brothers at the camp, they were shaking with fear. Their enemies had sent a giant named Goliath to attack them.

Every day, Goliath came out to the hillside across the valley and yelled ugly threats. He cursed God and His people. The giant laughed at the soldiers and dared them to fight him.

Goliath's words upset David.

"Why do you let him talk to you this way?" he asked the soldiers. "Why is no one standing up to this big bully? I will fight him myself!"

Now David's brothers were not only frightened—they were also angry and embarrassed that their little brother had more courage than they did.

"You're only a child," they said. "Go home and take care of your sheep."

Someone told King Saul about the shepherd boy who wanted to fight Goliath. The king himself was afraid to go onto the battlefield. He told David it was far too dangerous for a young boy.

But David insisted.

"Once when I was taking care of my father's sheep, we were attacked by a lion—and another time by a bear," David told the king. "But God rescued me. He gave me the strength to defeat the lion and the bear, and I know He will help me defeat this giant."

When King Saul saw that David had made up his mind, he let him go—but not without body armor! It was too big and heavy for a young boy, though, so David left it behind.

All by himself, David started across the valley to face Goliath. Along the way, he stopped by a little stream and picked up five smooth stones.

Goliath laughed when he saw the boy coming toward him. But David prayed that God would guide his hand. He put a small stone into his slingshot and aimed it at Goliath.

The stone hit the giant right in the middle of the forehead—and he fell at David's feet.

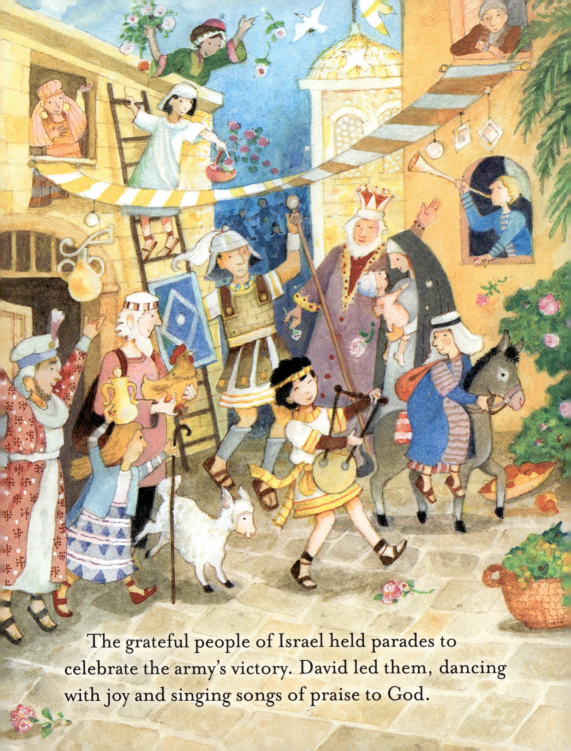

The grateful people of Israel held parades to celebrate the army's victory. David led them, dancing with joy and singing songs of praise to God.

This shepherd boy would grow up to be a brave and mighty warrior. As he led God's people into battle and defeated their enemies, David always asked God to show him what to do. And God was so pleased with David's courage and faith that He made David king.

All his life, King David continued to write beautiful songs of praise from his heart. Many of these songs, called psalms, are collected in the Bible. Thousands of years later, people all over the world still read and sing them today.